SIGNATURE GS

4 Modules That Let You Create a Computing Environment Uniquely Your Own

by *Duilio Proni*

Produced by:
Brian Wiser & Bill Martens

 Apple PugetSound Program Library Exchange

Signature GS

Copyright © 2019 by Apple Pugetsound Program Library Exchange (A.P.P.L.E.)
All Rights Reserved.

www.callapple.org

ISBN: 978-0-359-72017-0

ACKNOWLEDGEMENTS

Signature GS was programmed by Duilio ('D') Proni, with manual by Jerry Kindall, and was originally published by Quality Computers, Inc. in 1992.

This new manual, produced in coordination with Duilio ('D') Proni and Quality Computers president Joe Gleason, is released with their permission and is copyright by A.P.P.L.E.. Our thanks to Joe Gleason for kindly providing the licensing to create this re-production and for his support during the process.

The Cover and Book were redesigned by Brian Wiser.

PRODUCTION

Brian Wiser → Design, Layout, Editing, Art
Bill Martens → Scanning, OCR Conversion, Disk Updates

DISCLAIMER

About Duilio ('D') Proni

Duilio ('D') Proni purchased his first Apple II in 1981 and became obsessed with learning how to program so it could "do things." He received his B.S. in Computer Science from University of Central Florida in 1988. During this time he dabbled in writing shareware for the Apple IIGS along with commercial titles that were published by companies such as Quality Computers and Applied Engineering.

In 1990, he founded Econ Technologies, Inc. to produce internal hard drive systems and file management tools for the Apple IIGS. In the late 1990s, Econ shifted its focus to contract software development, but returned its attention to Apple in 2001 with the release of several commercial software titles for Mac OS X. Duilio continues to run Econ Technologies to this day, producing the the popular *ChronoSync* utility for macOS as well as *InterConneX* for iOS.

About the Producers

Brian Wiser

Brian Wiser is a long-time consultant, enthusiast and historian of Apple, the Apple II and Macintosh. Steve Wozniak and Steve Jobs, as well as *Creative Computing, Nibble, InCider,* and *A+* magazines were early influences.

Brian designed, edited, and co-produced many books including: *Nibble Viewpoints: Business Insights From The Computing Revolution, Cyber Jack: The Adventures of Robert Clardy and Synergistic Software, Synergistic Software: The Early Games, The Colossal Computer Cartoon Book: Enhanced Edition, What's Where in the Apple: Enhanced Edition,* and *The WOZPAK: Special Edition* – an important Apple II historical book with Steve Wozniak's restored original, technical handwritten notes.

He passionately preserves and archives all facets of Apple's history, and noteworthy related companies such as Beagle Bros and Applied Engineering, featured on AppleArchives.com. His writing, interviews and books are featured on the technology news site CallApple.org and in *Call-A.P.P.L.E.* magazine that he co-produces. Brian also co-produced the retro iOS game *Structris*.

In 2005, Brian was cast as an extra in Joss Whedon's movie *Serenity*, leading him to being a producer and director for the documentary film *Done The Impossible: The Fans' Tale of Firefly & Serenity*. He brought some of the *Firefly* cast aboard his Browncoat Cruise and recruited several of the *Firefly* cast to appear in a film for charity. Brian speaks about his adventures to large audiences at conventions around the country.

Bill Martens

Bill Martens is a systems engineer specializing in office infrastructures and has been programming since 1976. The DEC PDP 11/40 with ASR-33 Teletypes and CRT's were his first computing platforms with his first forays in the Apple world coming with the Apple II computer.

Influences in Bill's computing life came from *Byte* magazine, *Creative Computing* magazine, and *Call-A.P.P.L.E.* magazine as well as his mentors Samuel Perkins, Don Williams, Joff Morgan, and Mike Christensen.

Bill is a co-producer of many books including *What's Where in the Apple: Enhanced Edition, The WOZPAK: Special Edition, Nibble Viewpoints: Business Insights From The Computing Revolution,* and co-programmer for the iOS version of the retro game *Structris.* He has written many articles which have appeared in user group newsletters and magazines such as *Call-A.P.P.L.E.*.

Bill worked for Apple Pugetsound Program Library Exchange (A.P.P.L.E.) under Val Golding and Dick Hubert as a data manager and programmer in the 1980s, and is the current president of the A.P.P.L.E. user group established in 1978. He reorganized A.P.P.L.E. and restarted *Call-A.P.P.L.E.* magazine in 2002. He is the production editor for the A.P.P.L.E. website CallApple.org, writes science fiction novels in his spare time, and is a retired semi-pro football player.

Contents

Quality Computers

What is Signature?   1

Signature GS is a collection of Control Panel Devices (CDEVs) that make your Apple IIGS easier and more fun to use by adding a Screen Blanker, a Sound Selector, a Desktop Pattern Editor, and a Boot Setup Utility to your Apple IIGS. It runs under System Software 5.0 or later and works best with a hard drive. The full Signature package is simply too large to fit on a 3.5" disk along with the System Software.

What's a CDEV, anyway? It's pronounced "See-Dev," and it's short for "Control Panel Device." (If you were abbreviating "Control Panel Device," you'd probably come up with something like "CPD." But the term originated on the Macintosh – which may tell you a thing or two about the Macintosh people.)

All right, so what's a Control Panel Device, then? This question is best answered by a trip to the Apple IIGS Control Panel. Boot your IIGS into the Finder (or any IIGS desktop program). Pull down the Apple menu and select Control Panel. The window that appears is divided into two sections. Click an icon in the left section to choose a CDEV, the control panel settings offered by that CDEV appear in the right section. Use the scroll bar in the middle of the window to scroll the list of CDEVs up and down. Now, isn't it nice to know those little icons are called CDEVs?

When you install Signature, four additional icons will appear in the Control Panel to allow you to configure the four Signature modules. You'll select and use the Signature CDEV icons the same as any other icons in the control panel.

Since Signature is designed for the IIGS , its features only work when you're running IIGS-specific desktop programs. Signature's features work in AppleWorks GS, Platinum Paint, and HyperStudio, but not in AppleWorks 3.0, Publish It! 4, or The Print Shop GS. (Even though The Print Shop GS is a IIGS-specific program, it doesn't use GS/OS or the IIGS desktop.) Of course, you must also be in a desktop program if you want to access the Control Panel to configure the Signature modules.

PHANTASM

If you've lusted after the Mac's *Pyro!* or *After Dark*, you'll love *Phantasm*. *Phantasm* automatically blanks your screen after a period of inactivity to reduce the possibility of screen burn-in. (If you leave a static image displayed on your screen for a long period of time, it can get "burned" into your monitor. Then you'll see a "ghost" of the image when you're using other programs. You may even be even to see the image when the monitor is turned off!) *Phantasm* provides a colorful animated display instead of a mere blank screen-this reminds you that the computer is still turned on, while still protecting you against permanent burn-in damage. Plus, it's more fun.

SONICS

Sonics lets you assign sounds to certain IIGS system "events." You can change not only your system beep-you can even add sounds to disk ejections and insertions, keystrokes, error messages, and more. Sonics can play one sound when you start the computer and another when you shut it down. Use any digitized sound (including *HyperStudio* sounds and sounds converted from the Macintosh) – we've included a few to get you started. Sonics is more than just fun, it actually enhances your computer's functionality by providing unique, audible indicators for specific tasks.

GRAFFITI

That old baby-blue (the technical term is periwinkle) desktop can get boring after a while. The Macintosh has a built-in way to change the desktop's background pattern. Now, with *Graffiti*, the IIGS does too. Select any of *Graffiti's* solid colors or patterns, or design your own pattern with any of sixteen colors. It's a great way to personalize your IIGS desktop.

Boot Master

Boot Master is a true power user's tool that allows you to choose which GS/OS system components (including desk accessories, CDEVs, and drivers) are active on your IIGS. It's a big help in eliminating program conflicts and saving memory. You can even save "snapshots" of your system configuration for future use, plus get info on system file memory usage.

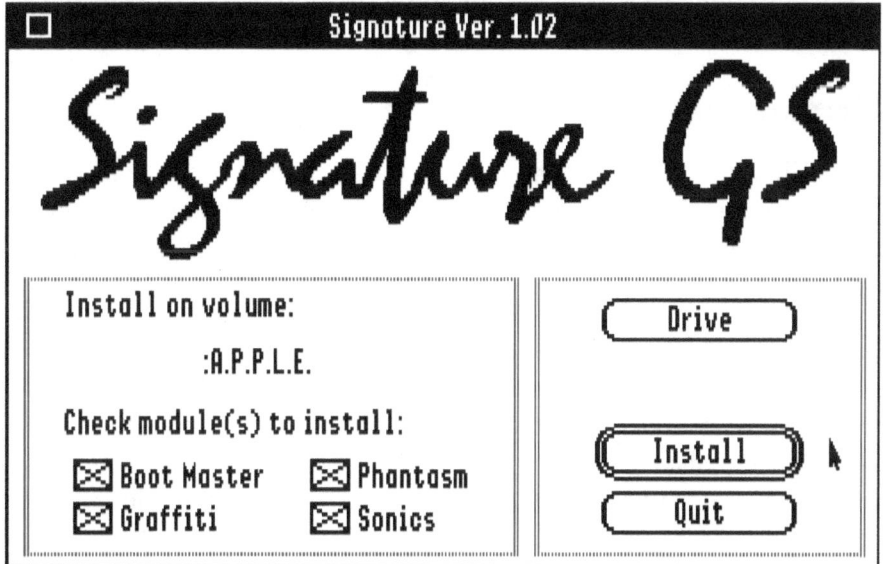

A disk image of *Signature GS* can be freely downloaded from the publisher's site: www.callapple.org. *Signature's* Installer does all the dirty work of putting the *Signature* CDEVs where they belong on your boot disk. To use the Installer, boot your system as you usually do. Then insert the *Signature* disk in any available 3.5" drive. The *Signature* icon will appear on your Finder screen. Double-click it to launch the *Signature* Installer. (If you don't use the Finder, your hard drive management system should have a way to run this program from the *Signature* disk. Consult your hard drive management system's manual.)

Select Disk for Installation

The *Signature* Installer displays the name of the volume on which *Signature* will be installed-the disk you booted from. Check the displayed volume to make sure it's really the one you want to install *Signature* on. If it's not, click the Disk button (to switch to your next drive) until the name of the desired drive appears.

Select Modules to Install

Use the checkboxes on the *Signature* Installer screen to select which *Signature* modules you want to install. By default, all modules will be installed, so if you do want to install all modules, you're all set.

Perform Installation

Click the Install button to begin installation of the selected *Signature* modules. When installation has been completed, click Quit to restart your system. (*Signature* will become active once you've restarted.)

When you first install *Signature* you will notice that there are only two sounds in *Sonics* and one blanking effect in *Phantasm*. Don't worry, we've included a plethora of additional sounds and effects on the *Signature* disk. Simply use the "Add" button to find the sounds and effects you'd like to include in *Signature* and add them in.

3.5" Disk Users

Although *Signature* works best with a hard drive and 2 megabytes of memory, it can work in a number of configurations with two 3.5" disk drives and somewhat less memory. Keep in mind that every time you add a digitized sound to *Sonics*, or a blanking effect to *Phantasm* more disk space and memory will be required. Since there is not much room on a 3.5" diskette with the system software, you may have to select a smaller configuration that works best for you. For a smooth installation on a 3.5" boot diskette, you will want to follow these general steps:

1. Prepare the boot disk.
2. Install *Signature*.
3. Test the configuration and customize.

Preparing a 3.5" Boot Disk

For the best results, start with a clean copy of the GS/OS system disk (version 5.04 or later). In order to fit the *Signature* files onto the disk, you need to delete some of the unnecessary, or infrequently used files. Each of the *Signature* features need a certain amount of space:

Phantasm: 27k (CDEV) + 51k (INIT) = 78k

Sonics: 39k (CDEV) + 13k (INIT) = 52k

Boot Master: 42k

Graffiti: 31k

You do not need to install all of the *Signature* modules. You may opt to install only one or two of them. Add up the amount of free space needed for the modules that you wish to use in order to judge how many of the unnecessary files you need to delete from the system disk.

Files You Can Safely Delete From Your Disk

The entire /System.Disk/Tutorial folder and the /System.Disk/AppleTalk folder (assuming you are not using AppleTalk). Just drag them over to the trash and select Empty Trash from the "Special" pull-down menu.

Additional Files You May Delete

In the "Volume" directory:

* If you will not be launching BASIC programs, you may delete BASIC.SYSTEM and BASIC.LAUNCHER.

In the "Drivers" folder:

* If you are not using a 5.25" diskette drive, you may delete the AppleDisk5.25 file.

* If you are not using a Modem, you may delete the Modem file.

* If you are not using a Printer, you may delete the Printer, Printer. Setup, and ImageWriter files.

7

In the "System.Setup" folder:

- If you have a ROM 3 IIGS (1 meg on the motherboard), you may delete the file "TS2."

- If you have a ROM 1 IIGS (256k on the motherboard), you may delete the file "TS3."

In the "CDEV" folder:

- Any of these files which you would like to delete are fine, since you can access any of these functions by pressing CTRL-OPTION-ESC.

In the "Fonts" folder:

- You may delete any of the fonts which you do not think you will use. A suggested configuration is to delete all of the fonts except for the 10 point fonts.

Installing Signature to a 3.5" Boot Disk

1. Install your system disk in drive one and the *Signature* disk in Drive 2.

2. Turn the power to your computer on, or boot the computer on the system disk.

3. When you reach the Finder, launch the "Signature Installer" on the *Signature* disk.

4. Use the check boxes to select which of the *Signature* features you wish to install to your boot disk and click on the "Install" button.

   Signature automatically checks to see if you have enough room on the boot disk for the configuration you chose. Once the installation is complete, press the QUIT button. *Signature* automatically reboots the system. Keep in mind that you will always need to keep the boot disk in the drive while you are using your computer for *Signature* to operate properly.

When using the installer, it might seem as though you cannot get both *Sonics* and *Phantasm* onto the 3.5" disk at the same time. This is because the CDEVs take up quite a bit of room. The good news is that the CDEVs are only needed in order to customize the features of *Sonics* and *Phantasm*. To fit both on the disk at once:

1. Install one of the features (*Sonics* or *Phantasm*), then access the CDEV to set it up the way you want. For instance, customize the *Phantasm* sleep corner. Then, delete the CDEV – you will find them in the "/System.Disk/System/Cdevs" folder.

2. Then install the other feature and repeat the process.

Testing the Configuration

To test the configuration, boot the newly-installed disk. When you reach the Finder, pull down the Apple menu and select "Control Panel." You should be able to scroll through the Control Panel Devices to see the CDEVs which you just installed.

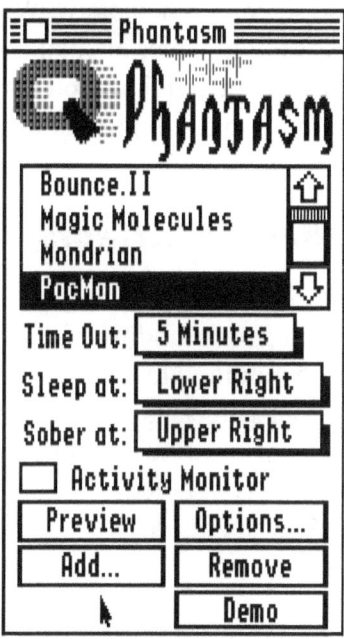

Phantasm lurks in the background of your computer's operation, activating itself automatically after a period of inactivity to prevent screen burn-in. Using the *Phantasm* CDEV, you can select and configure your favorite visual effect, the idle time before *Phantasm* activates, and other parameters.

To configure *Phantasm*, pull down the Apple menu and select "Control Panel." When the Control Panel appears, select *Phantasm* from the list of CDEVs.

Setting the "Time Out"

The Time Out pop-up menu tells *Phantasm* how much idle time it should let pass before taking over. If the Time Out period passes without keystrokes, mouse movement, or mouse clicks, *Phantasm* will "put your computer to sleep" and display the Effect you've selected. To "awaken" the IIGS, just move the mouse or press a key.

Setting "Sleep At" & "Sober At"

Use these two pop-up menus to define *Phantasm's* Sleep and Sober corners. When you move the mouse to the Sleep corner, *Phantasm* will blank the screen immediately. When the mouse is in the Sober corner, *Phantasm* will never blank the screen, even if the Time Out period passes without activity. You don't have to click the mouse, just move the pointer to the appropriate corner.

Configuring Individual Effects

The "Options" button is used to configure the individual Effects. When you click Options, a small window will appear with a few pop-up menus that can be modified to suit your taste. Figuring out how the Options affect your Effects is half the fun. In the Magic Molecules "Colors" menu, you can select more than one color. Colors with check marks are currently enabled – Magic Molecules will choose from these colors for its display.

Adding & Removing Effects

The "Add" button adds a new effect from a future *Signature* effects disk. The effects you select will be copied into the *Phantasm* CDEV. To delete an effect, click the "Remove" button. You might delete an effect to save disk space or to retire one you've grown weary of.

Previewing Effects

Use the Preview button to display a sample of the current Effect. (Move the mouse to "wake up" the computer.) The "Demo" button displays a one-minute sample of each of the installed Effects in sequence. (Not all Effects support the Demo button.)

Under System 5.0, *Sonics* allows you to assign sounds to the following Apple IIGS system events. (Under System 6.0, *Sonics* supports even more events. System 6 events appear as "gray" or disabled events when *Sonics* is used under System 5.0.)

Startup	Disk Insert	Caution Alert	Random
Shutdown	Disk Eject	Note Alert	Heartbeat
Restart	Keystroke	Stop Alert	Beep
Launch			

The sound you assign to the Beep event replaces the usual IIGS "bonk" beep. Heartbeat sounds are played repeatedly every few seconds. And Random sounds are played whenever the computer feels like it. Startup sounds are played during boot up. Other sounds are played when the event they're assigned to happens (e.g. a Caution Alert appears on the screen, or a key is pressed). To configure *Sonics*, pull down the Apple menu and select "Control Panel." When the Control Panel appears, select the Sonics CDEV.

Assigning Sounds to Events

To assign a sound to an event, pop up the Event menu and select the event. The sound currently assigned to this event will appear highlighted in the Sound list. To change the sound, just select the new sound (or "No Sound") from the Sound list. (You can assign the same sound to more than one event, if you want.) If you're just fooling around and only want to listen to sounds, select "Sound Test" from the Event menu. Clicking the speaker icon auditions your selected sound.

Adjusting Volume & Frequency

Clicking the Up and Down arrows to the left of the speaker icon adjust the volume of the selected sound. The arrows to the right of the speaker icon adjust the sound's frequency (pitch). *Sonics* remembers these settings for each event you've assigned a sound to, so even if you're using the same sound for two different events, you can set a different volume and frequency for each event.

Adding & Removing Sounds

Sonics comes with 26 sounds already installed. You can add more sounds from virtually any kind of sound file, including files created by *HyperStudio* and by Applied Engineering's Sonic Blaster and Audio Animator digitizers. To remove a sound, first click the sound in the Sound list, then click Remove. Events which used to use the removed sound are set to "No Sound."

Using Graffiti 6

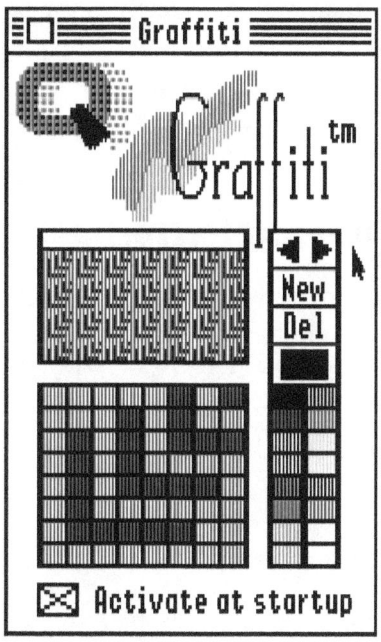

Graffiti lets you change your desktop background to virtually any color or pattern. To configure *Graffiti*, pull down the Apple menu and select "Control Panel." When the Control Panel appears, choose the Graffiti CDEV.

Choosing a Pattern

Use the Left and Right arrow icons to browse through *Graffiti's* built-in patterns and colors. Each pattern appears in *Graffiti's* preview window and fatbits editor. To make a pattern the active desktop pattern, click in the preview window. If you're in the Finder when you activate a new desktop pattern, the Finder icons will disappear. (The Finder doesn't quite know what to do when you put "wallpaper" over it.) The Finder icons are really still there-to reveal them, just click once where each used to be.

Changing a Pattern

If you don't like one of *Graffiti's* built-in patterns, you can change it or re-colorize it. Just choose the pattern you want to change with the arrow icons, then pick a color from the selection on the right and "draw" in the fatbits editor (just below the preview window). Afterward, click in the preview area to make your new pattern the active pattern (see "Choosing a Pattern" above).

Adding & Removing Patterns

You can add new patterns to Graffiti too (there's no limit to the number of patterns you can have). Just click the "New" button and a fresh white pattern will be created. Then draw your new pattern using the tips in "Changing A Pattern" above. If you grow tired of a pattern, just click the "Del" button and it will be deleted.

When It Doesn't Work

In certain programs, particularly paint programs, *Graffiti* will seem not to work properly, either displaying the wrong colors or not displaying a custom desktop pattern at all. In these circumstances, the program is using its own "palette" (set of colors) instead of the built-in IIGS palette. Don't panic, this is normal. *Graffiti* works fine with programs that use the standard IIGS palette-nearly all do.

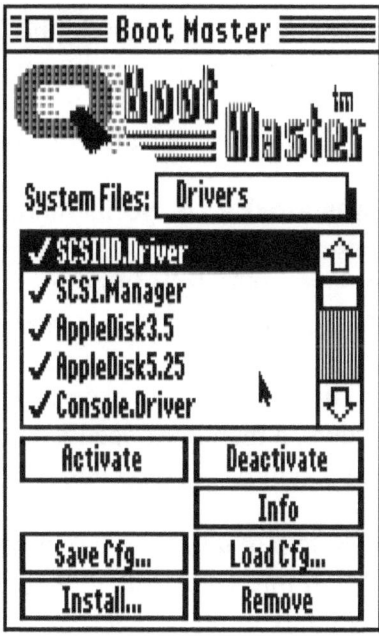

Boot Master isn't as glamorous as the other *Signature* modules, but that doesn't make it any less useful. GS/OS is a modular operating system-it keeps certain parts of the system (drivers, CDAs, NDAs, FSTs, INITs, and CDEVs) in separate files. *Boot Master* lets you turn any of these system components on and off whenever you want. If you don't use your 5.25" disk drives very much, for example, you might want to turn off the 5.25" driver to keep the Finder from grinding your empty drives.

To get to *Boot Master*, pull down the Apple menu and select "Control Panel." When the Control Panel appears, click the Boot Master CDEV to activate *Boot Master*.

Selecting a System File Type

Use the System Files pop-up menu to select which type of system files are displayed in the file window. *Boot Master* recognizes several kinds of system files.

Types of System Files

CDA (Classic Desk Accessory) – Appears in the menu you get when you press ⌘-Ctrl-Esc, accessible in any program.

NDA (New Desk Accessory) – Appears in the Apple pull-down menu, accessible only in GS/OS desktop programs.

CDEV (Control Panel Device) – We already know what these are.

FST (File System Translator) – A special module allowing GS/OS to access different types of disks. System 5.0 supports ProDOS, AppleShare, and High Sierra (CD-ROM) FSTs. System 6.0 supports all these FSTs plus Macintosh, DOS 3.3, and Pascal.

Inits – Programs which are loaded and executed at boot time. A PIF (Permanent Init File) stays in memory once loaded. A TIF (Temporary Init File) runs once and is removed from memory.

Drivers – Allow the system to talk to different types of devices. Printers, disk drives, MIDI interfaces, and other devices all require a driver before GS/OS will talk to them.

Activating/Deactivating System Files

Once you've selected a type of System File, the names of the appropriate files are displayed in the Files list. Active System Files have a checkmark next to their name. To turn a System File on, click its name in the Files list, then click "Activate." To turn one off, click "Deactivate" instead. You can also double-click a System File's name to toggle it from active to inactive and back.

Getting System File Info

Boot Master will tell you everything it knows about a particular System File, including how much space it occupies on disk and how much memory it takes up (if it's loaded) and when the file was created and when it was last modified. Just click the "Info" button.

Installing New System Files

If you get a new desk accessory or CDEV and want to install it on your boot disk, just select the appropriate type of System File from the pop-up menu and then click "Install." *Boot Master* will ask you to locate the System File you want to install, and then it'll copy it to your boot disk, automatically placing it in the right folder.

Saving & Loading Configurations

Boot Master calls the state of your System Files at any one time a "configuration." By clicking the "Save Cfg" button, you can create a snapshot of your system files at a moment in time. Later, when you want to return to the exact same setup, click the "Load Cfg" button. *Boot Master* will go through all your System Files and set them to the state (active or inactive) they had when you saved that configuration file. This is a great time saver if you have an INIT that doesn't work with a particular program, or a driver that's not compatible with a certain NDA, or any such incompatibility.

Remember to Reboot

Since System Files are loaded only at boot time, you must reboot for the changes you make in *Boot Master* to take effect.

What if I Turn Off Boot Master?

If you accidentally turn off *Boot Master* (or the Control Panel NDA or the CDEV Init), you won't be able to get to *Boot Master* again to turn it back on. Whoops! But all is not lost. Using the Finder, open your boot disk, then open the System folder, then open the CDEVs folder. Find *Boot Master*, then press ⌘-I. In the window that appears, click "Inactive" to reactivate *Boot Master*, then close the window. If you turned off the Control Panel NDA or the CDEV Init, open the "Desk.Accs" or "System.Setup" folder, respectively, and follow the same procedure to reactivate them, too.

Appendix: ProDOS File Types

Here are the three-letter file types originally defined in Apple's "About Apple II File Type Notes" tech note. In the first alphabetical list, we have weeded out filetypes that you are unlikely to encounter these days on the Apple IIGS. The list afterwards is organized by category.

In many file types, the file's auxiliary type is used to distinguish between one type of document and another. For example, in the LBR file type ($E0), aux type $8002 means that the file is a *Shrinkit* (NuFX) document. Auxtype $800C means that the file is a *Crypt* encrypted file. Both are displayed generically as LBR files in many programs. Graphics, sound, and many other "generic" filetypes are divided similarly.

File types $F1-$F8 are user-definable – any program can use these file types for any purpose.

Type	Hex	Description
8IC	$2C	Apple II Interpreted Code
8LD	$2D	Apple II Language Data
8OB	$2B	Apple II Object Code
8SC	$2A	Apple II Source Code
ADB	$19	*AppleWorks* Database
ANI	$C2	*PaintWorks* animation
ANM	$5B	Animation file
ASP	$1B	*AppleWorks* Spreadsheet
ATK	$E2	AppleTalk data
AWP	$1A	*AppleWorks* Word Processor
BAD	$01	Bad blocks file
BAS	$FC	Applesoft BASIC program
BDF	$AD	Apple IIGS BASIC data
BIN	$06	Binary data or program code
BIO	$6B	PC Transporter BIOS

CDA	$B9	Classic desk accessory
CDV	$C7	Control Panel device
CFG	$5A	Configuration file
CMD	$F0	BASIC command
COM	$59	Communications file
DBM	$D8	*DB Master* document
DIR	$0F	Folder (subdirectory)
DOC	$BF	GS/OS Document
DRW	$53	Drawing
DVR	$BB	GS/OS Device Driver
DVU	$5E	Development Utility
EDU	$56	Educational data
ENT	$5D	Game/entertainment document
EXE	$B5	GS/OS shell application
FND	$C9	Finder data
FON	$C8	Font
FOT	$08	Apple II packed graphics data
FST	$BD	GS/OS File System Translator
FTD	$42	File Type Descriptors
GDB	$52	Apple IIGS Database
GDP	$54	Apple IIGS Desktop Publishing document
GSB	$AB	Apple IIGS BASIC program
GSS	$51	Apple IIGS Spreadsheet
GWP	$50	Apple IIGS Word Processor
HDV	$6F	PC Transporter hard drive volume
HLP	$58	Help file
HMD	$55	Hypermedia document
ICN	$CA	Icons
INS	$D6	Instrument
INT	$FA	Integer BASIC program (also *Beagle Compiler*)
IVR	$FB	Integer BASIC variables (also *Beagle Compiler*)
LBR	$E0	Archival library (*ShrinkIt*, *Crypt*, etc.)
LDF	$BC	Generic load file
LIB	$82	Apple IIGS library file

MDI	$D7	MIDI data
MUM	$5C	Multimedia document
MUS	$D5	Music sequence
NDA	$B8	New Desk Accessory
OBJ	$B1	Apple IIGS object code
OCR	$41	OCR Data
OOG	$C5	Object-oriented graphics
OS	$F9	GS/OS system file
P8C	$2E	ProDOS 8 Code Module
PAL	$C3	*PaintWorks* palette
PAS	$EF	Pascal area
PFS	$16	*PFS* document
PIC	$C1	Super Hi-res picture
PIF	$B6	Permanent initialization file
PNT	$C0	Packed Super Hi-res picture
PRE	$6E	PC Transporter pre-boot
R16	$EE	EDASM 816 relocatable file
REL	$FE	Relocatable code
RTL	$B4	GS/OS run-time library
S16	$B3	GS/OS application
SCR	$C6	Script
SND	$D8	Sampled sound
SRC	$B0	Apple IIGS source code
STN	$57	Stationery
SYS	$FF	ProDOS 8 application or system file
TDF	$AC	Apple IIGS BASIC TDF
TDM	$20	Desktop Manager document
TDR	$6D	PC Transporter driver
TIF	$B7	Temporary initialization file
TOL	$BA	Apple IIGS Tool
TXT	$04	ASCII text
UNK	$00	Unknown filetype
VAR	$FD	Applesoft BASIC variables
WP	$A0	*WordPerfect* document

$0x Types: General

$00   UNK   Unknown

$01   BAD   Bad Block

$02   PCD   Pascal Code

$03   PTX   Pascal Text

$04   TXT   ASCII Text
              Auxiliary type is 0 for a sequential
              text file or the record length for a
              random-access text file.

$05   PDA   Pascal Data

$06   BIN   Binary File or Program Code
              Auxiliary type is binary
              file's loading address.

$07   FNT   Apple III Font

$08   FOT   Hi-Res/Double Hi-Res Graphics

$09   BA3   Apple III BASIC Program

$0A   DA3   Apple III BASIC Data

$0B   WPF   Generic Word Processing

$0C   SOS   SOS System File

$0F   DIR   ProDOS Directory

$1x Types: Productivity

$10   RPD   RPS Data

$11   RPI   RPS Index

$12   AFD   AppleFile Discard

$13   AFM   AppleFile Model

$14   AFR   AppleFile Report

$15   SCL   Screen Library

$16   PFS   PFS Document

$19	ADB	AppleWorks Database
$1A	AWP	AppleWorks Word Processing
$1B	ASP	AppleWorks Spreadsheet

$2x Types: Code

$20	TDM	Desktop Manager File
$21	IPS	Instant Pascal Source
$22	UPV	UCSD Pascal Volume
$29	3SD	SOS Directory
$2A	8SC	Source Code
$2B	8OB	Object Code
$2C	8IC	Interpreted Code
	$8003	– Apex Program File
$2D	8LD	Language Data
$2E	P8C	ProDOS 8 Code Module

$4x Types: Miscellaneous

$41	OCR	Optical Character Recognition
$42	FTD	File Type Definitions

$5x Types: Apple IIGS General

$50	GWP	Apple IIGS Word Processing
	$5445	– Teach
	$8001	– DeluxeWrite
	$8010	– AppleWorks GS
$51	GSS	Apple IIGS Spreadsheet
	$8010	– AppleWorks GS
$52	GDB	Apple IIGS Database
	$8010	– AppleWorks GS
	$8011	– AppleWorks GS Template
	$8013	– GSAS

$53	DRW	Drawing Object Oriented Graphics
		$8010 - AppleWorks GS

$54	GDP	Apple IIGS Desktop Publishing
		$8002 - GraphicWriter
		$8010 - AppleWorks GS

$55	HMD	HyperMedia
		$0001 - HyperCard GS
		$8001 - Tutor-Tech
		$8002 - HyperStudio
		$8003 - Nexus

$56	EDU	Educational Program Data

| $57 | STN | Stationery |

| $58 | HLP | Help File |

$59	COM	Communications
		$8010 - AppleWorks GS

| $5A | CFG | Configuration |

| $5B | ANM | Animation |

| $5C | MUM | Multimedia |

| $5D | ENT | Entertainment / Game |

| $5E | DVU | Development Utility |

$6x Types: PC Transporter

$60	PRE	PC Pre-Boot

| $6B | BIO | PC BIOS |

| $66 | NCF | ProDOS File Navigator Command File |

| $6D | TDR | PC Driver |

| $6E | PRE | PC Pre-Boot |

| $6F | HDV | PC Hard Disk Volume |

$7x Types: Kreative Software

$70	SN2	Sabine's Notebook 2.0
$71	KMT	
$72	DSR	
$73	BAN	
$74	CG7	
$75	TNJ	
$76	SA7	
$77	KES	
$78	JAP	
$79	CSL	
$7A	TME	
$7B	TLB	
$7C	MR7	

$7D   MLR Mika City
        $005C – Script
        $C7AB – Color Table
        $CDEF – Character Definition

$7E	MMM	
$7F	JCP	

$8x Types: GEOS

$80	GES	System File
$81	GEA	Desk Accessory
$82	GEO	Application
$83	GED	Document
$84	GEF	Font
$85	GEP	Printer Driver
$86	GEI	Input Driver
$87	GEX	Auxiliary Driver
$89	GEV	Swap File
$8B	GEC	Clock Driver
$8C	GEK	Interface Card Driver
$8D	GEW	Formatting Data

$Ax Types: Apple IIGS BASIC

$A0   WP   WordPerfect

$AB   GSB   Apple IIGS BASIC Program

$AC   TDF   Apple IIGS BASIC TDF

$AD   BDF   Apple IIGS BASIC Data

$Bx Types: Apple IIGS System

$B0   SRC   Apple IIGS Source Code

$B1   OBJ   Apple IIGS Object Code

$B2   LIB   Apple IIGS Library

$B3   S16   Apple IIGS Application Program

$B4   RTL   Apple IIGS Runtime Library

$B5   EXE   Apple IIGS Shell Script Application

$B6   PIF   Apple IIGS Permanent INIT

$B7   TIF   Apple IIGS Temporary INIT

$B8   NDA   Apple IIGS New Desk Accessory

$B9   CDA   Apple IIGS Classic Desk Accessory

$BA   TOL   Apple IIGS Tool

$BB   DVR   Apple IIGS Device Driver

$BC   LDF   Apple IIGS Generic Load File
                $4001 - Nifty List Module
                $4002 - Super Info Module
                $4004 - Twilight Module
                $4083 - Marinetti Link Layer Module

$BD   FST   Apple IIGS File System Translator

$BF   DOC   Apple IIGS Document

$Cx Types: Graphics

$C0   PNT   Apple IIGS Packed Super Hi-Res Picture
      $0001 - Packed Super Hi-Res
      $0002 - Apple Preferred Format
      $0003 - Packed QuickDraw II PICT

$C1   PIC   Apple IIGS Super Hi-Res
      $0001 - QuickDraw PICT
      $0002 - Super Hi-Res 3200

$C2   ANI   PaintWorks Animation
$C3   PAL   PaintWorks Palette

$C5   OOG   Object-Oriented Graphics

$C6   SCR   Script

$C7   CDV   Apple IIGS Control Panel Device

$C8   FON   Apple IIGS Font
      $0000 - QuickDraw Bitmap Font
      $0001 - Pointless TrueType Font

$C9   FND   Apple IIGS Finder Data

$CA   ICN   Apple IIGS Icon File

$Dx Types: Audio

$D5   MUS   Music

$D6   INS   Instrument

$D7   MDI   MIDI

$D8   SND   Apple IIGS Audio
      $0000 - AIFF
      $0001 - AIFF-C
      $0002 - ASIF Instrument
      $0003 - Sound Resource
      $0004 - MIDI Synth Wave
      $8001 - HyperStudio Sound

$DB   DBM   DB Master Document

$Ex Types: Miscellaneous

$E0   LBR   Archival Library
           $0000 - ALU
           $0001 - AppleSingle
           $0002 - AppleDouble Header
           $0003 - AppleDouble Data
           $8000 - Binary II
           $8001 - AppleLink ACU
           $8002 - Shrinkit (NuFX)
           $800C - Crypt

$E2   ATK   AppleTalk Data
           $FFFF - EasyMount Alias

$EE   R16   EDASM 816 Relocatable Code

$EF   PAS   Pascal Area

$Fx Types: System

$F0   CMD   ProDOS Command File

$F1   OVL   User Defined 1
$F2   UD2   User Defined 2
$F3   UD3   User Defined 3
$F4   UD4   User Defined 4
$F5   BAT   User Defined 5
$F6   UD6   User Defined 6
$F7   UD7   User Defined 7
$F8   PRG   User Defined 8

$F9   P16   ProDOS-16 System File

$FA   INT   Integer BASIC Program
           Also Used by *Beagle Compiler*

$FB   IVR   Integer BASIC Variables
           Also Used by *Beagle Compiler*

$FC   BAS   Applesoft BASIC Program
           Auxiliary type is BASIC program's
           loading address, should be $0801.

$FD   VAR   Applesoft BASIC Variables

$FE   REL   EDASM Relocatable Code

$FF   SYS   ProDOS-8 System File

www.ingramcontent.com/pod-product-compliance
Lightning Source LLC
Chambersburg PA
CBHW020957180526
45163CB00006B/2403